C000226097

some ending
Ben Norris

VERVE
POETRY PRESS
BIRMINGHAM

PUBLISHED BY VERVE POETRY PRESS
Birmingham, West Midlands, UK
www.vervepoetrypress.com
mail@vervepoetrypress.com

FIRST PUBLISHED MAY 2019 / REPRINTED OCT 2019

Printed in Birmingham by Positive Print

ISBN: 978-1-912565-21-4

CONTENTS

for my family,
whatever shape we take

nightswimming
after R.E.M.

I ran to the bay
hard and long-spined
like someone was watching
a keen blade
through the beetroot streets
of a new place
hit the rails at the end of the fishing pier
did my best titanic
eyes shut   arms wide   the figurehead
at the prow of the city

remembered my granddad
the non-swimmer
his sleepwalk down
to the sea one night
in morecambe/swansea/
somewhere

how he loosened a boat from the bayside
eased like the too-tight knot of a tie
rowed out into a patient dawn
his craft a finger lightly pressed
on the creaseless shirt of the water

I imagined him coming to   oddly calm
his hydrophobia a distant second to his reason
smiling the smile my mum sometimes says I have
noticing his raincoat buttoned perfectly
over his long johns and night vest
realising how little choice he had
to resurface there

I sucked back the severn salt
rare drug for an inland man
tipped a wide-brimmed windswept smile downstream
gazed out towards weston-super-mare
ten miles to the south east
latin america just a little beyond it

if I'd my father's wrist for skimming stones
if I'd my mother's hope
I thought   and felt
my anchor fall

I.

some prayer

we went to church
not normally a place I would go but you'd asked
to make my mum feel better I said yes
it was cold and enormous and people whispered
and walked the wrong way on their feet
songs were sung in dead languages
I forgot to take my hat off and was admonished
we stopped for mulled wine on the way
and had to drink it at the bar because
all the tables were reserved even though
none of those people would arrive for hours
it was our first christmas together
I am not going to say family christmas
you had sainsbury's basics whisky as a mixer
and mum bought you a posh welsh one to drink neat
often the best whiskies are made in casks
that once had other things in them
sometimes this doesn't work and it tastes like
earth or petrol or a heavy duty sterilising product
that kills everything
my dad still can't say your name

it's difficult for children to pinpoint the exact moment they realise that nothing lasts forever but rather it slides into view like the silver wink of the sea as the family astra rounds the bend of a lincolnshire hill

of course I wasn't to know
as jason leathen and I
pretended at playing snooker
on a full size table
as dad shuffled clare and me
round the go-kart track
if only to get our money's worth
as grey day turned to grey night
and the adults all drank
and nobody thought to lament
the fact that the mums and dads
of netherfield colts fc (under 15s)
couldn't afford to go abroad
as our static caravan
terrestrial telly
chicken nugget weekend
trundled on like
a 70s fairground ride
that no one found exciting even then
as butlins spluttered into monday

of course I wasn't to know
that you were setting yourself on fire
letting yourself love him
for the first time

you probably had brunch
probably held hands
linked   kissed
with february lips
like a torn calendar

I wasn't to know
that one day this would find itself
in a happy poem

the only ethnic minority dentist in boston lincolnshire

there is a wooden plaque on the spare room wardrobe door that says
friends are like stars   you don't need to see them to know they're there
but it helps doesn't it   I am grateful that you said I could live with you
even though I won't it's nice to know I could   it cost you a lot to say
that I could tell   our love has to find a practical valve to escape from
perhaps because I am not your son or just that we are bad at it   perhaps
there is no other way we can love   your decorations are tasteless and
your dog is enormous and every room is either too hot or too cold   you
can see for miles here but there is nothing to look at   lincolnshire is a
famously flat county   there was a time I couldn't sleep in the spare room
because your clothes were on the bed and this was non-negotiable   you
are proud of having found the only ethnic minority dentist in boston
lincolnshire   statistically the most racist town in britain if you take
brexit as a measure of racism which we all do   not that you were looking
I do not know how you voted in the referendum and I am not going to
ask   you hate all geordies because your ex-husband's new wife has a
geordie accent so I'm not confident   you drive a cobalt blue subaru
impreza forty years too young for you with a personalised number plate
of your old married name   you ask questions about my life you want to
hear the answers to even though you know the answers might be things
you have no interest in don't really understand or actively dislike   you
touch my dad's back as if he is a boy in his early to mid twenties and you
are a girl in your early to mid twenties and you have taken him home to
meet your parents and your parents have just left for half an hour and
you are allowed to put your hands on him properly for the first time   I
never knew he had this joy in him   I like watching you both wash up
neither of you thought you would have a second chance   you don't have
unlimited broadband but I sleep naked here now and sometimes hang
my clothes up when I stay

[anything other than myself]

[i remember] st. john's wort in the kitchen
nestled in the bread bin not hidden [exactly]
but not asking to be found as if it knew
[the questions] that would come
[i would] make toast on my tiptoes
and [think] how can anyone just *be* sad?
your dressing gown is soft and you have a job
and so does dad and he doesn't hit you
even if his breakfasts are boring
at his doctor's insistence [i thought]
because I had things to look forward to
everyone had things to look forward to

[i feel like] I have an itch in the middle
of my back that I can't quite reach
and the itch is my [phantom] sadness
and my hands are other people's love

[i keep] waiting to calm down

if you lived here you would be home by now!

we both struggle with seasonal affective disorder
in the winter you have to generate your own warmth
you can't just sit there and stay alive

everyone says I am entertaining
[i try and] remember the last time [i made myself laugh]
is it like saturday night tv
when there were only three channels
and nowhere else to be or is it like
a compilation of people pissing
themselves at bus stops as captured
on council security cameras

a millennial falling down an escalator phone first
a little boy on a stool fixing a breakfast
of instructions and possible side effects
while his mum ignores a tea and tries to feel
differently

high-quality clinical evidence is lacking

why is all of this only coming out now?

[when i was ten] you tried to leave him
halfway round the world from his meagre friendships
a trip you didn't want him on in the first place
he didn't get out of bed [for months] just carried
his sadness to different climates as we worked
our [slow] way home you told us he had a cold

[when i was fifteen] you said maybe your dad
should've just been a one night stand and we both agreed
this was a good thing [for me to hear]

you must have spent so much time
on the ring road in those double years [those billboards]
did you ever think about not driving home
[did it still feel like driving home]

you were worried [i wouldn't know] what love is
like if you've never been shown the dark
how do you know darkness but [i can
close my eyes] if you've only ever had noise
can you imagine music but [i have]
put my fingers in my ears before now
[i have been to friends' houses]

none of this made you a bad mum

if you're going to mess something up
better to do it through too much love

[i had such a textbook childhood]

the first poem [i wrote] about your affair
was positive [i was so desperate]
to be okay with everything I arrived at the answer
without any of the working I showed the therapist
[i wouldn't need] for another seven years
such [formidable] progress I have always been
more concerned with being impressive
than being okay standing at a crossing
and [waving] through a train

there is [surely] more to life than tolerating
things I think of my childhood
with diplomatic neutrality like [i'm trying
to be] the bbc even shame was better than this
but maybe you have to feel nothing
before you can feel something again

I have never pretended to be
any surer than curious I have never
pretended to be [anything other than myself]

if you lived here you would be home by now!

we have a saying in the family after I burst
a three kilogram bag of oats by tearing not cutting
despite your repeated warnings it's called
a *muesli moment* when something is inevitable
and disastrous and is going to take a fuck of a long time
to clean up but you do it anyway
because you gotta eat

sister

when we were both table height
you called me a name too much like school
locked the kitchen door so I kicked it in
kicked the word from your mouth
and your tooth came too so confusing
to regret something as you're doing it
I was in my tears before you were in yours
but feeling guilty in another room is not
the same as saying sorry grandad said
you might as well knife her

*

you've gone the full bart simpson
call our parents by their first names
like colleagues to whom you're indifferent
met on a team building exercise
built a clumsy foam bridge in some woods
then shared a silent train back
to the city texting your chosen people

*

you make statements like
we're not a close family
spending christmases now
in places where christmas
doesn't exist – except the
christmas you said you were done
with us all but I didn't believe you
you were crying too much
to be done

*

we do practical things now
split each other's leftovers
in flats we each share with strangers
and their boyfriends talk about
the past as little as possible
you built my website
and probably also the poster
for the gig at which
I will first read this poem

*

writing this is not the same
as saying thank you

*

I went to see you graduate
visiting a place you loved
only once you were leaving
everything mattered less to you
our parents standing far apart
in the few photos we took only half of them
coming for lunch I wanted to get pictures of
us you wanted to get
pictures with friends

*

I never know whether to put kisses
at the end of our texts

*

we had a semi-detached childhood
you stopped being naked around the house
escaping mortified to the en suite in the roof
as soon as the conversion was done
moved everything upstairs and
made me feel disgusting
the way I got out of bed and
cleaned myself
the way I woke up

*

your friend showed me her boobs once
in a two-person game of spin the bottle
we were so young it was like looking
in the mirror I was only excited because
I felt I should be

two funerals

I've witnessed one of these -hugs-
mum grabbing at the stopped clock of dad's arms

she'd say
-we're really getting somewhere-
-today I held him-
when of course she always has

a woman who measures progress
in the amount of times
he let her look at him
or dropped a muscle-memory
joke

or how she touched him
when of course she never stopped
but he doesn't want to be
reminded of that cruel tenancy
that squatter in his heart

enduring her salesman haste
and brittle chipper grin
trying to flog him normalcy
like a recorded message
an accident that wasn't your fault?
trying to flog him penance

if to have -a hug- is to sell the house and draw
a hard line he'd say then a hug will be had
the final hurdle jumped
us two kids now the only thing

between them   like a sheet
between them   standing
at opposite ends holding
flapping and folding us
making a bed for lying in

you can be wronged and wrong at the same time

nan's funeral was so empty
even the professionals
looked uncomfortable
-just the three pieces of music
is it sir? and no speaking sir?
that's fine sir it's your day-
even though it wasn't
anybody's

if he could have burned her
without ceremony he would have
what a waste of petrol

I took my double grief to the pub   a wake
with a completely different set of people
was asked   -how was it?-   -*was it?*-
and all I could do was talk about what hadn't happened

two selfies

i. *with her*

the snappy adolescent still
shouting down the stairs
it's amazing how quickly
our heads draw back
into the shells of youth
she still wants to mother me
and I hate that I hate that
a need to prove
I am okay without her
which is still a need for her
to know I'm okay clenched
fist of boyhoods on the sofa

ii. *with him*

I'm calmer never thought
I would feel like this around
a man I convinced myself
I was so unlike and a dog
still learning my smell
feeling uneasy does not mean
feeling unwelcome I'm still
lynx africa for christmas
but at least I'm something
for christmas how sublime to have
someone to roll your eyes at
people without love
don't roll their eyes

- - - - - - - - -

II.

donuts *or* aubade for boys

at the all-male office
donuts meant sex
meant they'd had her

a sweet treat for the lads
to slap the morning
on its hairy back

the rich boys
bought a dozen
per woman

fit to burst with sugared fat
packing packed
with the ugly stuff

we don't want to want
I didn't know yet
what donuts meant

and we'd gather
round like beasts
to gorge on the fall

as if the body itself
were laid on the table
glazed and unboxed

as if we'd all been there
cheering from the sidelines
snacks in hand

glued ringed
stuffing gaps
into our big mouths

two portraits

i. *everything boy*

ii. *big shy boy*

short shorts and big jumpers
big show and no show
arrogant shy boy
sticks out chest then punctures
takes burst balloon to room
patient as a kettle
wants kisses deep and hard
except with her
tiny mouth with her
wants to eat himself
toy car on a wall
pull-back-and-go
brakes
and walks
GSOH
lives entirely outside of body
constantly worrying about body
like watching self on CCTV
little fat skinny boy
stuffing face
trying not to get caught
like he's broken into
his own house

big shy boy
big little clown
in his small trousers
five foot something
depends who's asking
life and soul mostly
does as told mostly
the kind of boy
who comes with warnings
the kind of boy who warns
depends who's asking
careful
he might disappear
or want touching
two bathtubs for feet
just because he talks for a living
doesn't mean he wants to
little shy boy listening
little soft boy
big man
needs a lie down
needs to go now

porn

quicker than a shag and never
letting someone down   no dance of wants
or endless drinks and pep talks in the toilet
instead the slap and gag of someone else's cock
in someone else's throat   the staying home
the sounds-like-fun of it
a barbeque in a neighbour's garden
nice car crash on a dashboard cam
on channel 5 in the slippy hours
wet wipes on the side and no one died

they're asking for more   listen
when do we ever beg for things
we know are going to hurt us?

inheritance

when I miss you I think of koalas
not the cuteness or the clinging
or the slovenly chew
but the closeness   the stench
the fact that many have chlamydia
but still tourists hold them
the fact their sex sounds like
distressed machinery and chiefly
that their young consume
their mother's shit   the sheer
proximity   the trust that
they have eaten well enough
that whatever you put in your mouth
I will put in mine

I read the bloodaxe book of modern australian poetry

I read the bloodaxe book of modern australian poetry to try and feel closer
to you but it just makes me feel further away and like a worse poet so I pour
a glass of australian wine which works a little better and look through this
small window at a distinctly british field wet with genuine rain   you water
your grass out there   you're coming on sunday and I'm hoping you won't
mind that our sun is seldom hot enough to bake the land but the sky is kind
enough to quench it and deliver me you   gift wrapped in silver and sleep
half a dozen films deep   sent from the future   -does it get any better?-
I'm not proud of the things that I want but I'm not ashamed for wanting
them   for him to be happy elsewhere   for your mother to know my name
they tell us when we're little if we dig deep enough we'll get there   I am trying
to train myself out of saying sort-of-girlfriend

fox

you are seven megapixels
held in the palm of my hand
I read you bits of fantastic mr fox
to help you sleep nine hours
and fifteen years ahead

your hand is difficult to hold
when you're wearing his ring
a city I cannot find my way around
our fingers have to rest limply
like the touching is an accident
like we might be commuters
reaching for the same handrail or
how a leaf catches briefly on a gate
nothing can take root here

the fox necklace I gave you
is the kind of thing that might be
gifted by a sibling
worn openly at dinner
with his parents or
hidden by a shirt

a ring is something different
the body bends to give and take
something always seen

the stakeout is what kills me
the waiting and the waiting
and the hiding til they almost starve

signal

I've taken a week away to miss you
put down my phone and so your body
as if to look away a minute
is to remember you more clearly
a you that is already so gone
I am bent double with it
sketching the space in a photograph
you've been cut out of
your head on my chest   there
your hand on my side   there
like my ribs are the grip on a racquet

I walk to the top of the hill
to at least the second cattle grid they said
if you want signal   then howl the space
across the devon afternoon   this bit of england
I don't know   a sound that makes the animals uneasy
like a sheepdog at the coming of a storm
and all the cows lie down
and I lie with them
until only my body can speak
tell you the size
and shape of my need

we only ever talk of losing weight
not of how or where to find it

in the film of this moment

in the film of this moment I would
jump the barriers despite having
my oyster card in my pocket
catch your sagging back as it sinks
down to platform level tell you I was wrong
I was wrong and that the sadness in my eyes
is connected to an actual sadness it is not
a performance

          but the film of this moment
would be a performance and I would not
play myself I am not the body flinging itself
at a second or third chance because love
is a commitment to not know together
the tfl station attendant shouting *some ending!*
  I am the body walking away and we are
  two flat tyres on different bikes
                  in different lives

at home I find the fox on the bedside table
half hidden beneath the fall of chain
it looks like it's leaping from a tangle of branches
like it's trying to escape itself

better the devil

reading the PTSD page of the NHS website
I feel my first relief in thirty weeks if you're going
to go mad go the kind of mad
that someone knows

III.

curiosity and opportunity

a mars rover learnt
to sing itself happy birthday
because if you're all alone how else
are you going to celebrate but things that didn't happen
probably cannot have anniversaries

> [I think there is a poem about self care in this
> after all isn't everyone picking up rocks
> looking for a reason for a party but
> the thought sits gathering dust
> 138 million miles away]

a mars rover said
'my battery is low and it's getting dark'
before it finally lost contact with nasa
built for ninety days lived for fifteen years
but things that weren't born probably cannot die

makeup artist

I thought you might kiss me
I have never been so close to someone
that I didn't love than when
you fixed my face   eyes looking
everywhere but mine   the land
between us staying neutral   staying
sacred   I half expected your hands
on my waist but you were just at work
and good at it   you worked fast
and were gone   on to take the shine
off someone else's nose   it is easier
to love someone you don't yet know
and to write about someone
you don't yet love

some ending

I have come to america to write because you made a library here
invited me to sit in it and see what happens   so far it's me and
lots of dead ladybirds and ladybirds flying into windows   I am doing my best
to tell them that what looks like the way out is often not the way out
it is late march now but the grass is still brown   it is difficult to distinguish
between grass that has burned and grass that has drowned
and grass that has held under months of snow
but it seems ready to begin living visibly again

a man on a ride-on mower is cutting the brown
lack of grass   sometimes just feeling useful is useful
it is not always a bad idea to plan
a welcome home party for something
you're not sure is coming back

*

[there are a lot of different yous in this thing
I realise this must be confusing   so was the writing
and the living   baffled as someone trying to swim in several pools
at once   there are so many people to apologise to   I am not sure
it's possible to eat from a spinning plate   I was never
a very good bartender but if you want a metaphor mixing I'm your man

*

I'm nobody's man   I want my relationships to feel
like things that build not things that stick
I need to love people better not more
and not more people   one of those people

32

is definitely myself   how is it possible
to have been so selfish and so unhappy
don't answer that   there's a reason
we have stopped talking]

*

in paris they had to remove a decade
of padlocks from the pont des arts
because it was collapsing under
all that wishful thinking
even forever cannot last forever
the replacement glass is already covered in graffiti
like the top stone at black rocks
or the trunk of every stubborn tree in every public park
when we've tattooed our skin we take to the land
carving our love into things that will outlive it
this is about wilful destruction
of historic places said the local paper
padlocks or pens it's the same sickness: ego
people wouldn't do this in their hometowns
except they do

*

a friend has bought a cheap lumi lamp equivalent
one of those lights that rouses you slowly
the body she says doesn't like to be shocked awake
a fake sunrise is a real sunrise
if it gets you out of bed
it depends what you think
the morning is for

----

a plenary question for victorian medical practitioners and their ancient predecessors concerning the role of the organs and humours in the governance of feeling

tell me   who decided that the heart is where love lives?
I have sent fifty beating red emojis this week
to friends in distress and people I want
to say thank you to   people I am missing
people I missed   a new friend is listening to silences
differently   an old friend is helping her   I feel a displacement
tell me   where is the small intestines emoji   I can't very well
send you the little poo and expect you to know what I mean
where is the insomnia emoji   the glowing yellow
person staring into a fridge not hungry just empty
you have given us this new language but
no language to talk about it   tell me
what is the emoji for safety   what is the emoji for
thank you: I didn't know how to say any of this before

SOME ACKNOWLEDGEMENTS

Thanks are due to the editors of the following publications and programmes, in which some of these poems first appeared: *Bare Fiction, Two Words For, The Emma Press Anthology of Love, Popshot* and BBC Radio 3's *The Verb*.

Several of these poems were written on residencies at Totleigh Barton and Olio House respectively. I am grateful to Andrew McMillan, Caroline Bird, and all the other writers for an inspiring and provocative week in Devon, to the Think Olio gang for letting a stranger sit in their loft in Wassaic, and to Bianca - playmate and puncture repair extraordinaire - for inviting me there and helping me to find the space to do this.

Thank you to Stuart, for publishing this, and for being such a tireless champion of new writers, particularly us from the Midlands. Thank you to Andrew McMillan and Jo Bell for your feedback on these poems, and to all who have read previous drafts. Thank you to the 78 Bournbrook, Writers' Bloc, and UOB crews for incubating this dream in the first place, and to Bohdan Piasecki for helping to hatch it.

With deepest love to my Mum, Dad, Clare, Sue and Brian. Thank you for putting up with being in so many poems, the difficult ones as well as the happy ones.

To my friends, in particular Bianca, Connor, Jack, Oscar, Siobhán, Rachel, Sean, Jess C, Beth, Nadi, Kez, Bohdan, Mair, Jess G, Scott, and Joss. And to Peta.

'two funerals' is in memory of my Nan.

The section of 'some ending' beginning 'in paris...' features quotes taken from the article "From padlocks to pens: Loved-up tourists graffiti iconic Paris bridge" in *The Local* , 6th October 2017.

ABOUT THE AUTHOR

Ben Norris is a poet, playwright and actor. He is two-time national poetry slam champion and regularly appears at literary festivals, music festivals, and poetry and spoken-word nights up and down the country, from Latitude to the Proms at the Royal Albert Hall. His work has been broadcast across BBC Radio, his debut solo show, The Hitchhiker's Guide to the Family, won the 2015 IdeasTap Underbelly Award at the Edinburgh Fringe Festival, and his first short film, commissioned by Channel 4, was nominated for a Royal Television Society Award. He has also written commissions for Southbank Centre, IdeasTap, RHS, and Ditch the Label, among many others.

Ben was born in Nottingham and studied at the University of Birmingham before training at the Royal Welsh College of Music and Drama. He is currently poet-in-residence for Nottinghamshire Libraries, Creative Associate at Nottingham Playhouse, and is a former writer-in-residence at Theatr Clwyd.

some ending is his second pamphlet of poems.

ABOUT VERVE POETRY PRESS

Verve Poetry Press is a new press focussing intently on meeting a local need in Birmingham - a need for the vibrant poetry scene here in Brum to find a way to present itself to the poetry world via publication. Co-founded by Stuart Bartholomew and Amerah Saleh, it is publishing poets from all corners of the city - poets that represent the city's varied and energetic qualities and will communicate its many poetic stories.

Added to this is an experimental and spoken pamphlet series featuring poets who have previously performed at the festival, and a debut performance poetry series, which will see us working with the brightest rising stars on the UK spoken word scene.

Like the festival, we will strive to think about poetry in inclusive ways and embrace the multiplicity of approaches towards this glorious art.